Contents

The arrangements on pages 2 through 13 are in the key of A (3 sharps), and can be played by **lever harps tuned to the key of C or flat keys, and pedal harps**.
You will need sharping levers on C, F, and G strings.

Pages 14 through 25 are in the key of G (1 sharp), and can only be played by **lever harps tuned to 1, 2 or 3 flats, and pedal harps**.
You will need sharping levers on F, and B strings.

How to choose the right arrangement

#1. If you tune your lever harp to the key of C, play the arrangements on pages 2 and 6.

#2. If you tune your lever harp with at least one flat, you can play any of the arrangements. If you choose the arrangements on pages 14 and 18, you will set fewer levers before you begin than you would need for the versions on pages 2 and 6. This may mean that your harp will sound better.

#3. If you play pedal harp, you can play any of the arrangements.

Lever changes are written between the treble and bass clefs. Pedal changes are below the bass clef.

Solo harp arrangements

The arrangements on pages 2 and 14 are for solo harp. There are many places in the music where one string is played by both hands in the same measure. For example, in measure 2 the initial melody note in the right hand is played again by the left thumb 3 notes later. Because of this, you won't be able to place your left thumb at the beginning of the measure. Whenever this happens, try to let each string ring as long as possible before placing. Also, be sure that the melody notes are louder than the accompaniment throughout.

As an optional variation, when you return to measure 2 for the D.S. al Coda, you can play the right hand an octave higher in measures 2 through 8.

Harp and melody duets

The arrangements on pages 6 and 18 are for harp and voice or a melody instrument.

VOICE: The arrangements are for low or low/medium voice. Some of the higher notes are written with smaller noteheads. These can be omitted if they are too high for the singer.

INSRUMENTS: Both arrangements work well on violin. There are some notes too low for the flute, but alternate notes are provided in the arrangements.

HARP: The melody part could also be played on a second harp, although no fingerings are provided. The melody may be played with one hand, as written, or in octaves split between right and left hands.

1

Unchained Melody

for lever harps tuned to the key of C or flat keys, and pedal harps

HARP SOLO

Lyric by HY ZARET, music by ALEX NORTH
Arranged for harp by SYLVIA WOODS

Lever harp players: set your sharping levers for the key signature, and then re-set the lever shown above.

Moderately slow

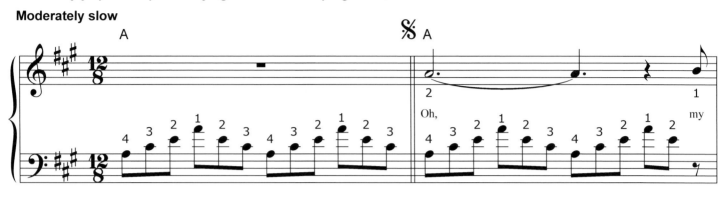

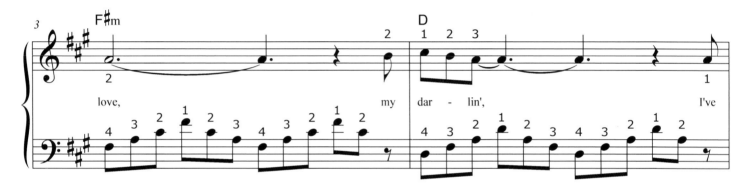

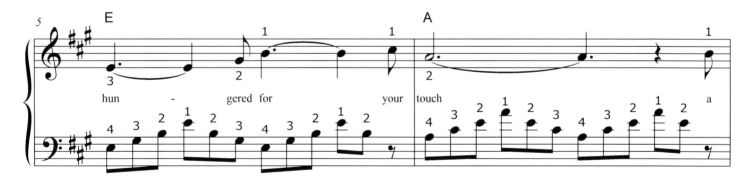

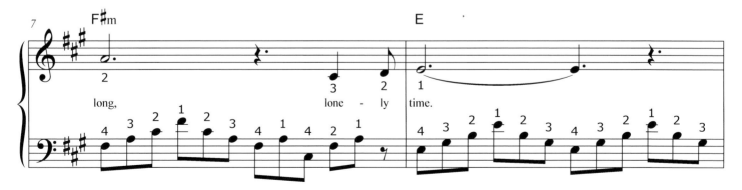

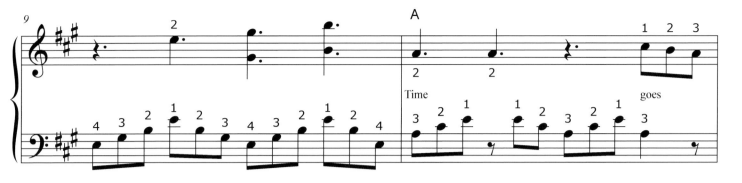

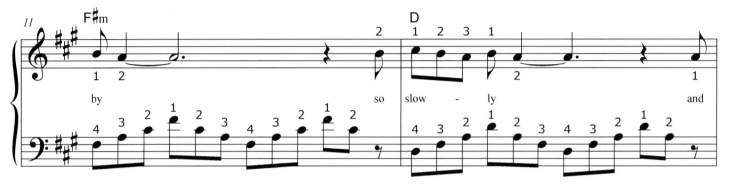

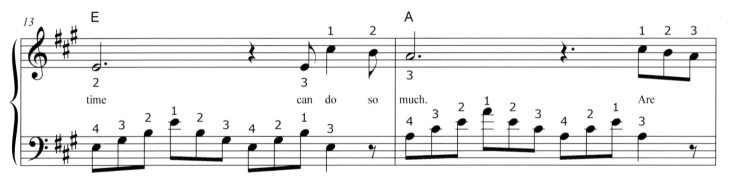

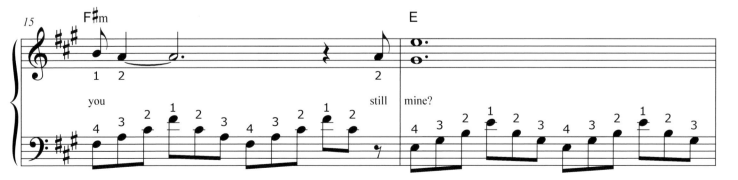

For the page turn, you may play many of
the LH notes in this measure with your RH.

I need your love.

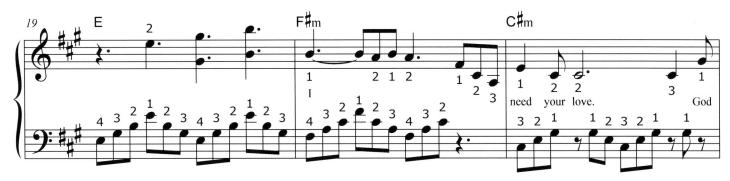

I need your love. God

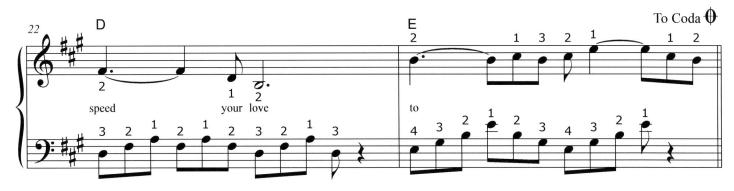

speed your love to

To Coda

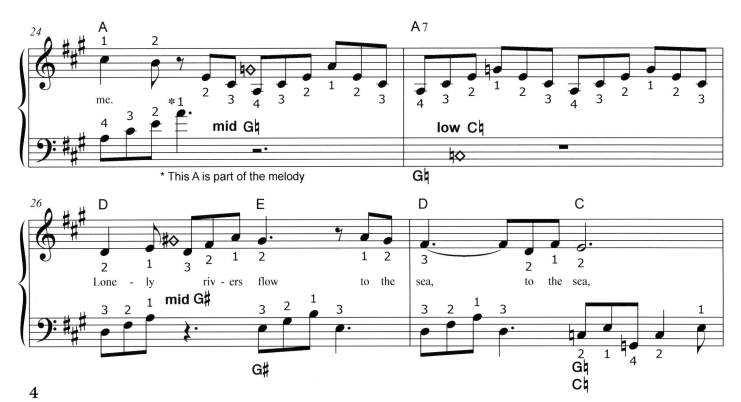

me.

mid G♮

low C♮

G♮

* This A is part of the melody

Lone - ly riv - ers flow to the sea, to the sea,

mid G♯

G♯

G♮
C♮

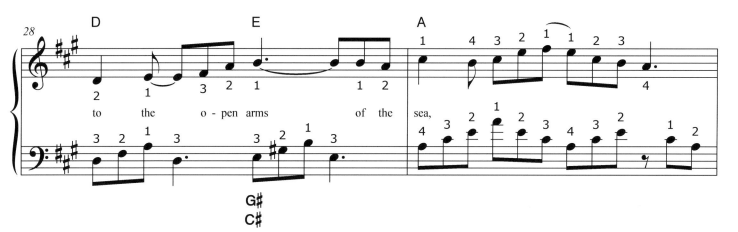

to the o - pen arms of the sea,

G#
C#

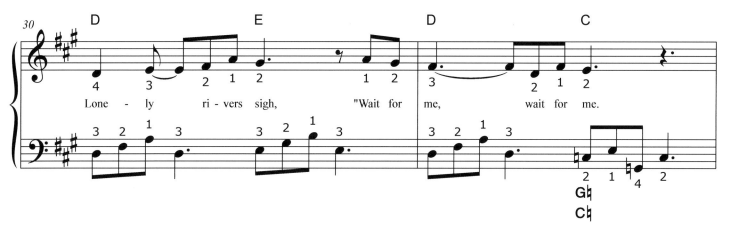

Lone - ly ri - vers sigh, "Wait for me, wait for me.

G♮
C♮

D.S. al Coda

I'll be com - in' home. Wait for me!"

low C#

G#
C#

* This A is part of the melody

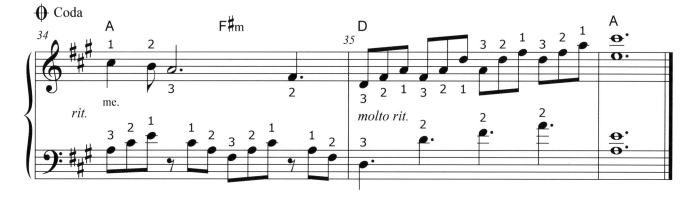

Coda

A   F#m   D   A

rit.   me.

molto rit.

5

Unchained Melody

for lever harps tuned to the key of C or flat keys, and pedal harps
HARP SCORE for HARP & MELODY DUET

Lyric by HY ZARET, music by ALEX NORTH
Arranged for harp by SYLVIA WOODS

This duet arrangement is for all types of harps, along with voice, flute, violin, or other melody instrument.
The melody part could also be played on a second harp.

In measure 22, there a B directly below middle C in the melody. Flute players, and other instruments with middle C as their lowest note, should play the alternate measure printed above measure 22.

Notes with small noteheads in measures 17 and 29 are optional if they are too high for the voice.

The melody part for instrumentalists and vocalists is printed on pages 12 to 13.

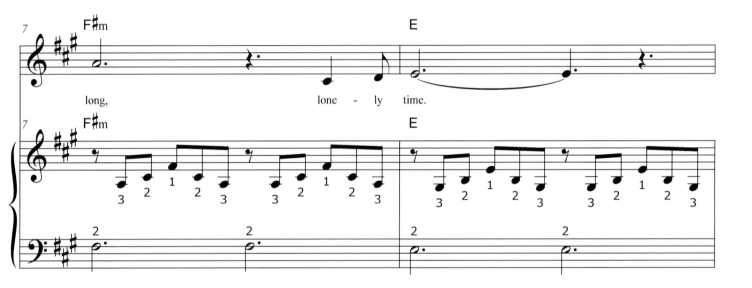

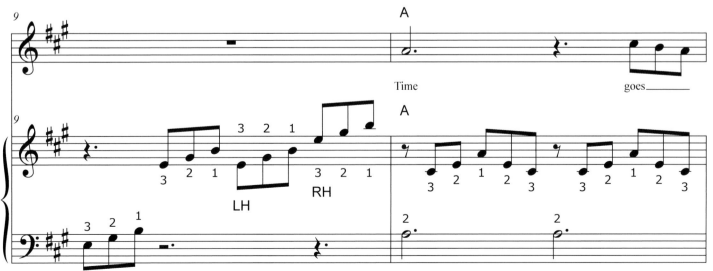

For the page turn, you may play one or both of these these LH notes with finger 4 of your RH.

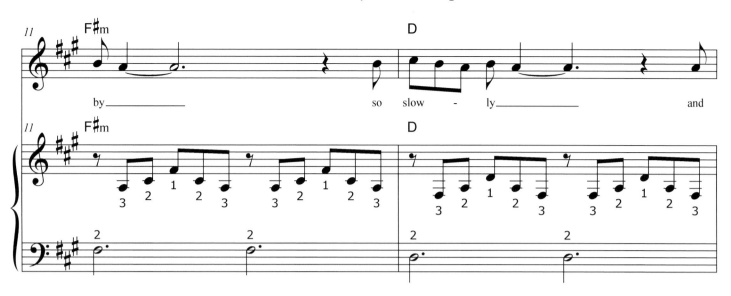

by _____ so slow - ly _____ and

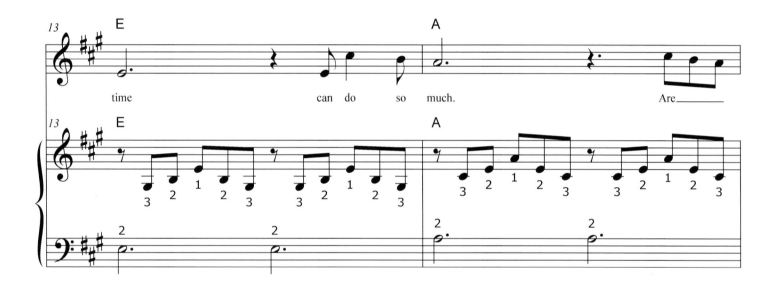

time can do so much. Are _____

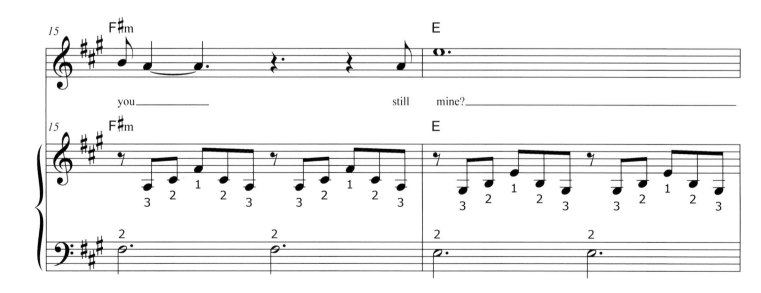

you _____ still mine? _____

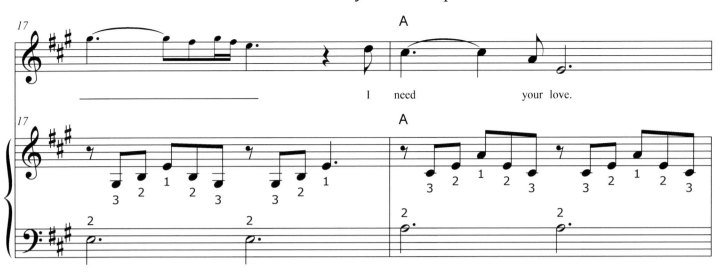

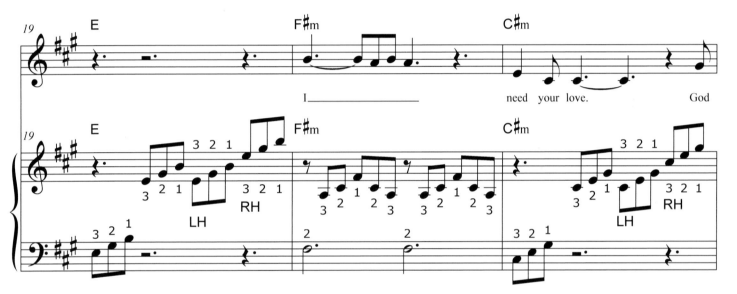

For the page turn, you may play one or both of these
these LH notes with finger 4 of your RH.

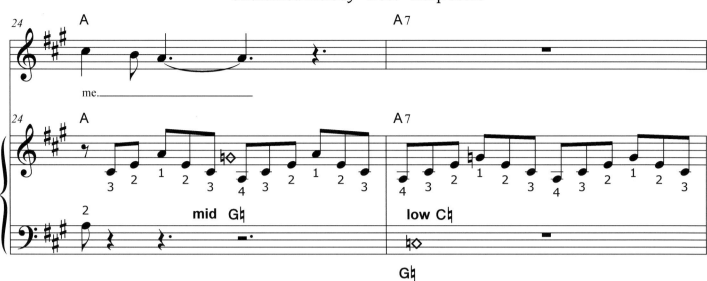

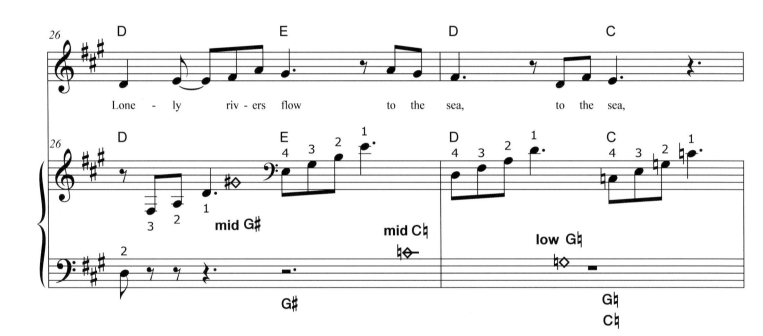

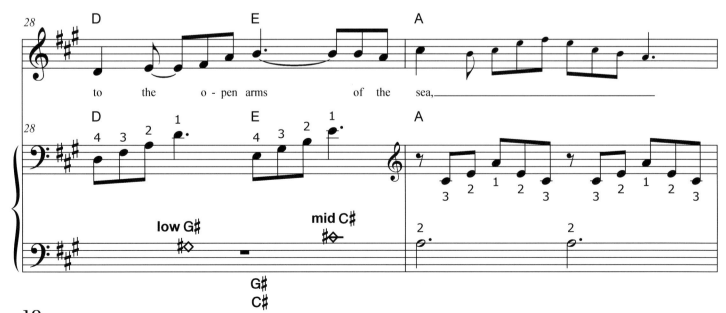

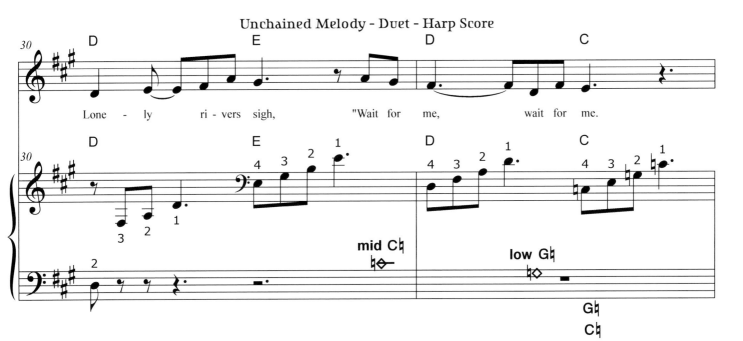

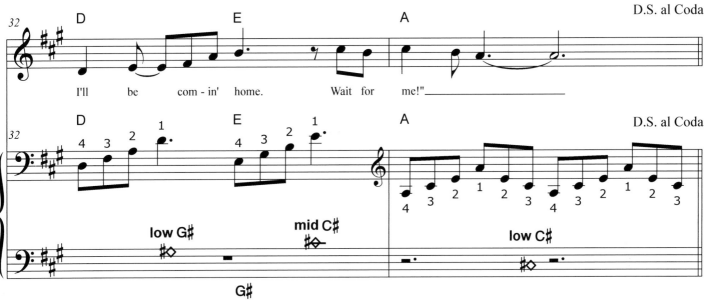

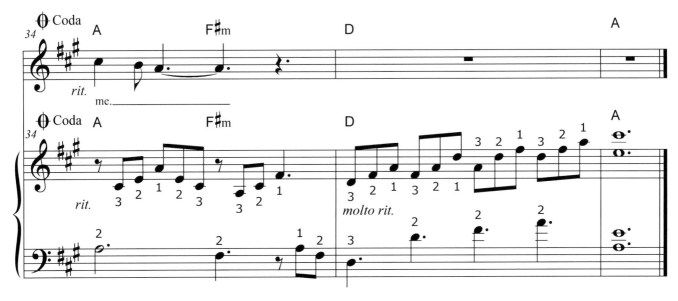

Unchained Melody

INSTRUMENTAL / VOCAL PART for HARP & MELODY DUET

Lyric by HY ZARET, music by ALEX NORTH
Arranged for harp by SYLVIA WOODS

This is the melody part for the harp score in the key of A starting on page 6.
It is for voice, flute, violin, or other melody instrument. It could also be played on a second harp.

If the lowest note on your instrument is middle C, play the alternate measure printed above measure 22.

Notes with small noteheads in measures 17 and 29 are optional if they are too high for the voice.

Unchained Melody

for lever harps tuned to 1, 2, or 3 flats, and pedal harps

HARP SOLO

Lyric by HY ZARET, music by ALEX NORTH
Arranged for harp by SYLVIA WOODS

Lever harp players: set your sharping levers for the key signature, and then re-set the lever shown above.

Moderately slow

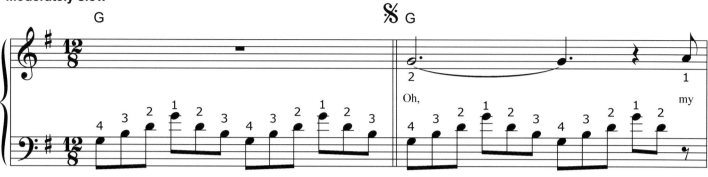

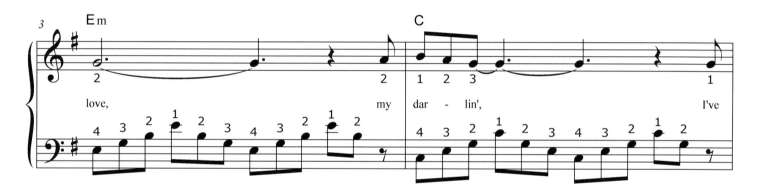

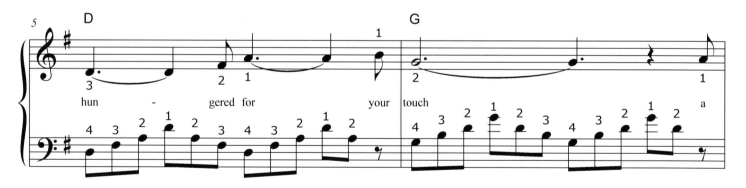

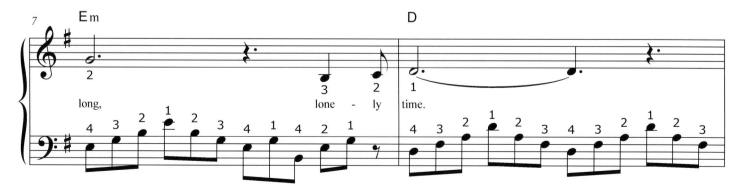

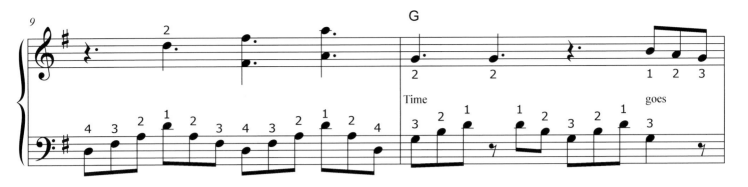

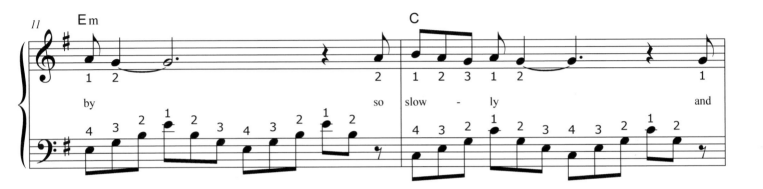

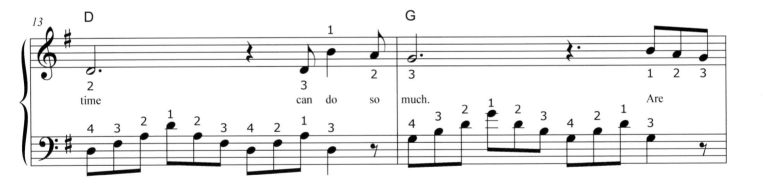

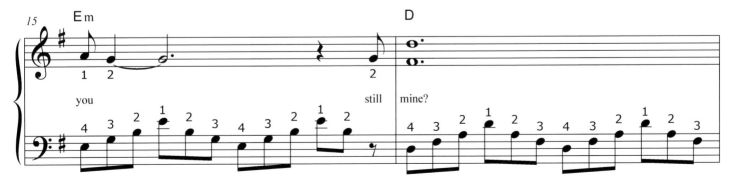

For the page turn, you may play many of
the LH notes in this measure with your RH.

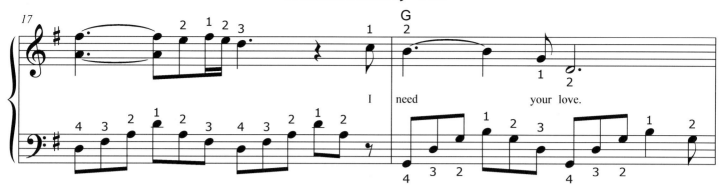

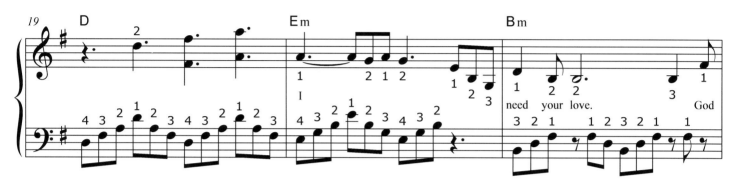

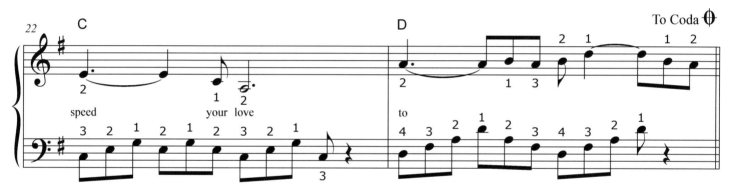

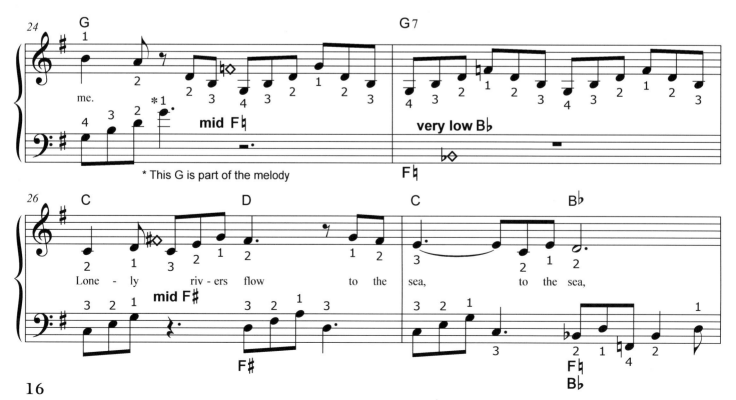

16

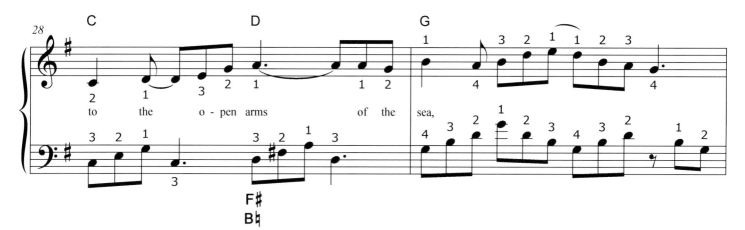

* This G is part of the melody

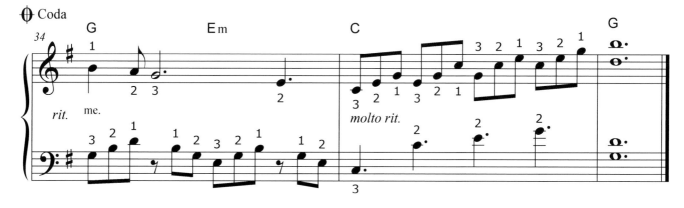

Unchained Melody

for lever harps tuned to flat keys, and pedal harps
HARP SCORE for HARP & MELODY DUET

Lyric by HY ZARET, music by ALEX NORTH
Arranged for harp by SYLVIA WOODS

This duet arrangement is for all lever harps tuned to flats and pedal harps, along with voice, flute, violin, or other melody instrument. The melody part could also be played on a second harp.

Notes with small noteheads in measures 17 and 29 are optional if they are too high for the voice.

The melody part for instrumentalists and vocalists is printed on pages 24 to 25.

Moderately slow

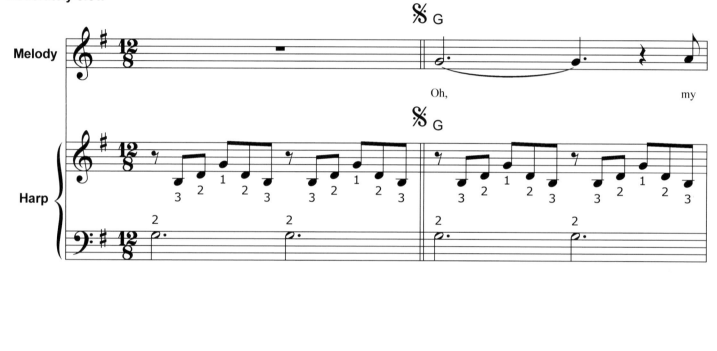

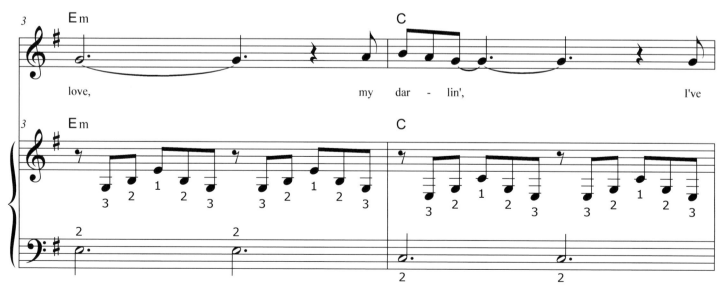

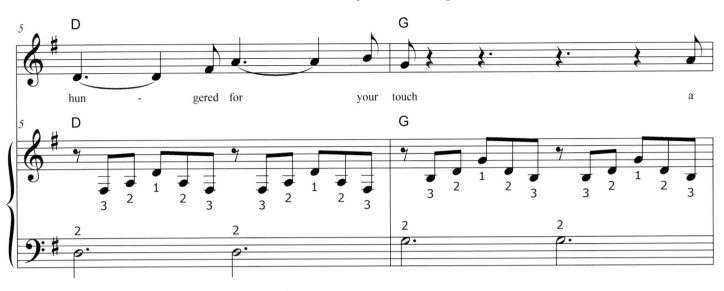

hun - gered for your touch a

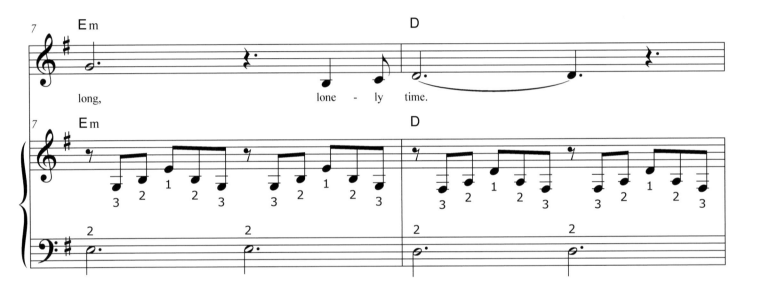

long, lone - ly time.

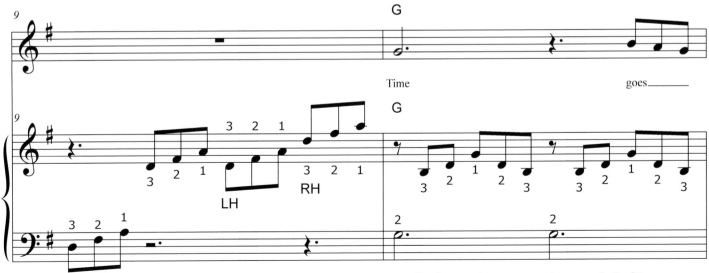

Time goes

For the page turn, you may play one or both of these
these LH notes with finger 4 of your RH.

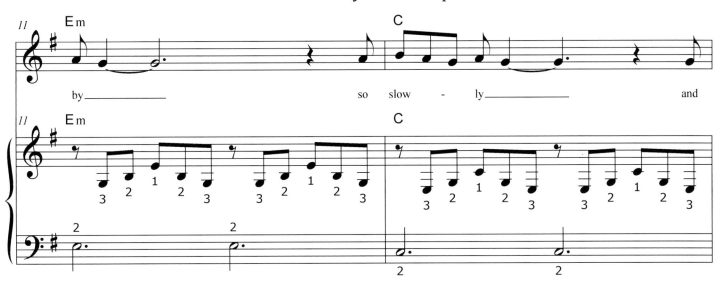

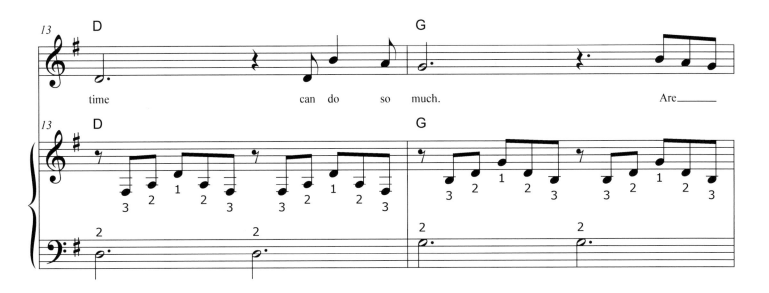

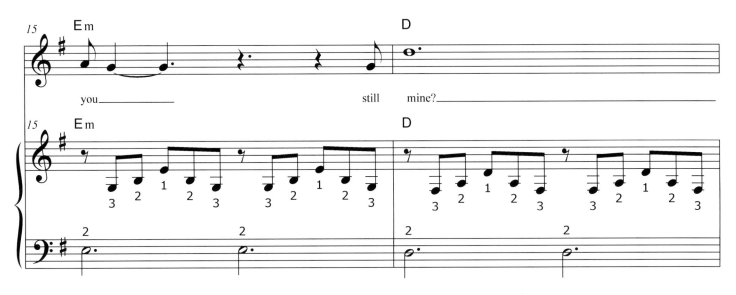

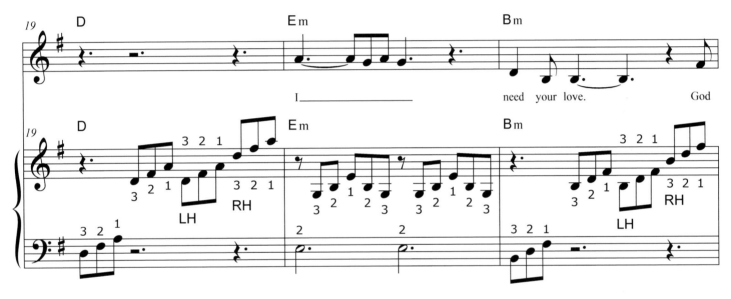

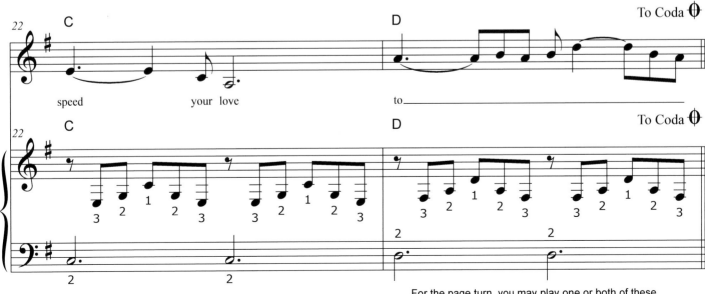

For the page turn, you may play one or both of these
these LH notes with finger 4 of your RH.

21

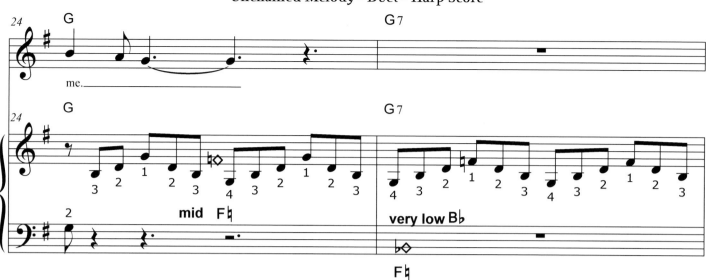

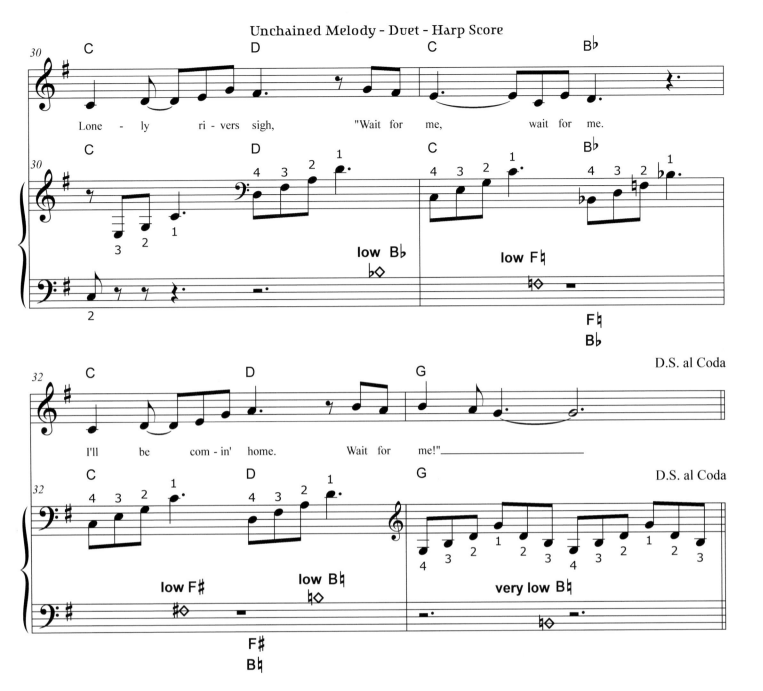

Unchained Melody

INSTRUMENTAL / VOCAL PART for HARP & MELODY DUET

Lyric by HY ZARET, music by ALEX NORTH
Arranged for harp by SYLVIA WOODS

This is the melody part for the harp score in the key of G starting on page 18.
It is for voice, flute, violin, or other melody instrument. It could also be played on a second harp.

If the lowest note on your instrument is middle C, play parts of measures 7-8 and 21-22 an octave higher than written, as indicated with the optional 8va.

Notes with small noteheads in measures 17 and 29 are optional if they are too high for the voice.